WITHDRAWN

Why were dinosaurs scaly?

First published as hardback in 2006 by
Miles Kelly Publishing Ltd, Bardfield Centre,
Great Bardfield, Essex, CM7 4SLCopyright
© Miles Kelly Publishing Ltd 2006

This 2009 edition published and distributed
by:

Mason Crest Publishers Inc.
370 Reed Road, Broomall, Pennsylvania
19008
(866) MCP-BOOK (toll free)
www.masoncrest.com

Why Why Why—
Were Dinosaurs Scaly?
ISBN 978-1-4222-1574-6
Library of Congress Cataloging-in-
Publication data is available

Why Why Why—?
Complete 23 Title Series
ISBN 978-1-4222-1568-5

Printed in the United States of America

Contents

What is a dinosaur?

Dinosaurs were animals that lived millions of years ago. There were lots of different types of dinosaur—little ones, big ones, fierce ones, and shy ones. All dinosaurs lived on land—and they died out a long time ago. There are no dinosaurs living today.

Make

Use salt dough or plasticine to make some dinosaur models. Use a picture or a toy dinosaur as a guide.

When did dinosaurs live?

It is thought that the first dinosaurs lived around 230 million years ago. They roamed the Earth for the next 165 million years, before becoming extinct (dying out) about 65 million years ago. Humans haven't been around for two million years yet!

Herrerasaurus

Where did the dinosaurs live?

Dinosaurs lived all over the world. At that time, the weather was much hotter than it is today. There were plants such as ferns, mosses, and large evergreen trees, but there were no flowers.

What a terror!

The word "dinosaur" means "terrible lizard," even though dinosaurs weren't lizards! Many of the plant-eating dinosaurs were about as terrible as today's sheep!

Did any dinosaurs eat plants?

Many dinosaurs ate plants. *Plateosaurus* grew up to 26 feet long. It had a long neck and could reach high up into trees by standing on its back legs. It grabbed branches with the hooks on its thumbs and nibbled at the tastiest leaves.

Plateosaurus

List

Starting with the letter A, list plants that you eat. A could be for apple, B for banana and C for carrot.

Why were dinosaurs so big?

Riojasaurus (ree-oh-ja-saw-rus) was a giant dinosaur that measured 33 feet from its nose to the tip of its tail. Being tall meant that it could reach high into trees for food. Big dinosaurs could fight off enemies, such as *Rutiodon*, a big crocodile that lived at the time.

Riojasaurus

Rutiodon

No fruit!

Early plant-eating dinosaurs did not eat fruit or grass—none had appeared yet! Instead, they ate plants called horsetails, fern, cycads, and conifer trees.

Why did dinosaurs eat stones?

Lots of plant-eating dinosaurs swallowed their food without chewing. Instead, they gobbled stones and pebbles, which stayed in their stomachs. When they swallowed food, the stones helped to mash the food up, turning it into a pulp.

How big is a dinosaur tooth?

Dinosaur teeth were different sizes. Meat eaters, such as *Tyrannosaurus rex*, needed large, sharp and pointed teeth for tearing flesh. Each tooth measured up to 6 inches! When scientists look at dinosaur teeth they can work out what type of food the dinosaur ate.

Toothy!

Baryonyx had small, pointed, cone-shaped teeth. These are like the teeth of a crocodile or dolphin today. They were good for grabbing slippery food such as fish.

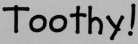

Did plant eaters need sharp teeth?

Plant-eating dinosaurs, such as *Apatosaurus*, had long, thin teeth that were blunt, not sharp. They used these teeth to pull leaves off branches. Herds of these dinosaurs could strip all the plants clean in one area, before moving on.

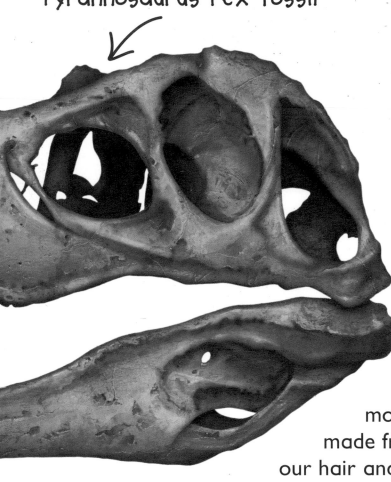

Tyrannosaurus rex fossil

Think

You have different types of teeth. Think about which ones you use to cut food, and which ones you use to chew.

Did all dinosaurs have teeth?

Not all dinosaurs needed teeth. *Ornithomimus* had a beak-shaped mouth without teeth. Its mouth was made from the same tough substance as our hair and nails. This bird-like dinosaur probably pecked at seeds, worms, and bugs. Its large eyes helped it to find food.

Ornithomimus

What were the biggest dinos?

The biggest dinosaurs, called sauropods, were **ENORMOUS!** Each one could weigh as much as ten elephants. *Brachiosaurus* was one of the largest dinosaurs that ever lived and was 82 feet long. It was twice as tall as a giraffe and could reach the tops of the tallest trees.

Draw

Lots of animals eat plants and live in groups, or herds. Draw some modern animals that spend all day eating plants.

Brachiosaurus

Argentinosaurus

What was the biggest dinosaur that ever lived?

The biggest dinosaur ever discovered is *Argentinosaurus*. Not much is known about this giant, but it is thought that it may have measured 130 feet from head to tail! *Argentinosaurus* had a huge body but a small head and brain.

Scary tail!

Diplodocus is also known as 'Old Whip-tail'! It could swish its tail so hard that it made a CRACK! like a whip. This would scare off enemies or even rip off their skin.

What did sauropods eat?

All sauropods ate plants. They probably had to spend most of the day eating, just to get enough energy for their enormous, heavy bodies. They may have spent 20 hours every day just grazing and nibbling at plants.

Why did dinosaurs have claws?

Most dinosaurs had claws on their fingers and toes. Meat-eating dinosaurs, such as *Deinonychus* (die-non-ee-kus) used their claws for catching and killing other animals. These dinosaurs were fast, clever and strong. Their claws could cut like knives and their teeth were razor-sharp.

Discover

Look at books to find pictures of elephants' feet. Do their toenails look like the claws of Apatosaurus?

Deinonychus

Apatosaurus

Claws

Were all claws sharp?

Even plant-eating dinosaurs, such as sauropods, had claws. They didn't need claws to catch other animals, so they were flat and blunt rather than sharp. *Apatosaurus* had claws to protect its feet from stones, just like nails protect your fingertips and toes.

Thumb nose!

When scientists discovered remains of Iguanodon, they found a bone shaped like a horn. They put this on Iguanadon's nose. Now they think it is a thumb claw!

Which dinosaur had a spike on each hand?

Iguanodon was a plant-eating dinosaur. It didn't need spikes to kill other animals, but it could use them as weapons to defend itself. If meat-eating dinosaurs attacked *Iguanodon*, it could fight back with its strong arms, using its spikes like daggers.

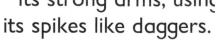

What was the scariest dinosaur?

Tyrannosaurus rex—known as T-rex for short—is one of the scariest dinosaurs. This dinosaur was a large meat eater. It had powerful legs that helped it run fast and a huge mouth filled with lots of sharp, pointed teeth.

Tyrannosaurus rex

Color

No one knows what color dinosaurs were. Draw your favorite dinosaur, then color it in using spots, stripes, and colors!

Giganotosaurus

What was the biggest meat-eating dinosaur?

Giganotosaurus was even bigger than *T-rex*—it is the largest meat-eating dinosaur ever found. Its huge legs could carry more than 8 tons of weight, even when it was chasing its prey. It had small arms and both had three claws for grabbing and stabbing.

How did meat eaters get their food?

Some meat eaters hunted and captured their prey using their powerful claws and sharp teeth. Others were scavengers. This means that they ate any dead animals that they found. It is thought that *T-rex* both hunted, and scavenged, for food.

Bite marks!

Some meat-eating dinosaurs not only bit their prey, but also each other! Remains of a T-rex had bite marks on its head. Perhaps the dinosaurs fought each other to become leader of the pack.

Which dinosaur had big eyes?

Dinosaurs used their senses to see, touch, hear, smell, and taste. *Troodon* was a bird-like dinosaur that had HUGE eyes. Scientists think it may have hunted at night, and that its large eyes helped it to find food in the dark.

Troodon

Play

Play a game of hide and seek. Use your senses, such as seeing and hearing, to hunt your prey!

What were the noisiest dinosaurs?

We can't be sure what sounds dinosaurs made, but *Parasaurolophus* was probably one of the noisiest! It had a large crest on its head that was made of hollow bone. *Parasaurolophus* could have blown air through the crest to make a bellowing noise, like a giant trumpet.

Parasaurolophus

Were dinosaurs clever or stupid?

Animals with big brains are usually cleverer than those with small brains. *Apatosaurus* had a tiny brain. *Troodon* had a large brain, compared to the size of its body. It may have been one of the cleverest dinosaurs that ever lived.

Dino rap!

Small meat-eating dinosaurs are called "raptors." These dinos lived and hunted in packs. They were slim, clever, and fast. Some even had feathers to keep them warm!

How fast could dinosaurs move?

Some dinosaurs could run very fast—up to 50 miles an hour. That is faster than a horse at full gallop! *Ornithomimus* could run this fast because it had a slim body, hollow bones, and long, thin legs. It ran fast so it could chase other animals, and escape being eaten itself!

Ornithomimus

Print

Dip feathers in paint and press them on paper to make your own prints. Try making handprints, too.

Could big dinosaurs move quickly?

Large dinosaurs were often slower. Heavy bodies were harder to move! *Muttaburrasaurus* was a big dinosaur that may have run on its hind legs, holding its head up to look for enemies. Its long tail may have helped it to keep its balance.

Muttaburrasaurus

Speedy!

Coelophysis (seel-off-ee-sis) could trot, jump and leap. It ran upright on its two back legs. It could also bound along on all four legs like a dog, at speeds of 18 miles an hour.

Were some dinosaurs small?

All dinosaurs were quite small when they first hatched from their eggs! Some fully-grown dinosaurs were not much bigger than a pet cat. *Compsognathus* was a small, light dinosaur that ate little creatures, such as lizards and bugs.

Were dinosaurs scaly?

Dinosaurs needed to protect themselves from their enemies. Some of them did this by growing great pieces of bone over their bodies. Scales, and these bony plates, protected the dinosaurs' soft bodies like huge shields or suits of armor.

Triceratops

Which dinosaur had a lumpy tail?

Euoplocephalus (you-o-plo-seff -a-lus) had a tail that was strengthened with lumps of bone. When this dinosaur swung its tail, it could hit an attacker with such force that it could break a leg!

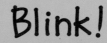

Blink!

The armored dinosaur Euoplocephalus (you-oh-ploh-sef-al-us) was so well-protected that it even had bony plates on its eyelids, which could snap open and closed, just like shutters!

Which dinosaur had three horns?

Triceratops was a plant eater and it probably used its three horns to frighten away attackers. It would also have used them for fighting enemies. *Triceratops* looked scary, but it probably spent most of its time quietly eating plants.

Styracosarus

Euoplocephalus

Protoceratops

Make

Make a dinosaur model from clay or dough and then add a suit of armor. Include horns and a tail-club, using cardboard or pebbles.

How did dinosaurs have babies?

Dinosaurs laid eggs, just like birds, lizards, and crocodiles do today. *Protoceratops* was a small dinosaur, the size of a pig. It lived in the desert. The female made a bowl-shaped nest in the warm sand and then laid her eggs inside it.

Find out

Find out how much you weighed and how long you were when you were born. Ask how quickly you grew!

Did dinosaurs look after their babies?

Some dinosaurs did look after their babies, until they were old enough to look after themselves. *Maiasaura* collected food for its newly hatched young and fed it to them, rather like birds feed their chicks today. The parents probably guarded their babies, too.

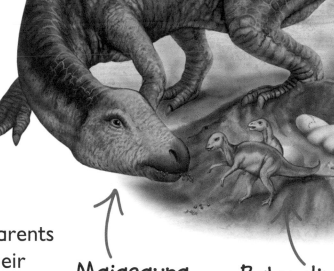

Maiasaura

Baby dinosaurs

Protoceratops

How do we know about dinosaur babies?

Scientists have found dinosaur eggs, and the remains of nests that have lasted for millions of years. They have even discovered large areas where many *Maiasaura* mothers came to lay their eggs, year after year.

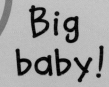

Big baby!

Baby dinosaurs grew up to five times faster than human babies! A baby dinosaur, such as Diplodocus, was already 3 feet long and 66 pounds in weight when it came out of its egg!

Did dinosaurs live alone?

Some dinosaurs lived alone, but many lived in groups, or herds. *Velociraptor* was a fast runner and meat eater that lived in packs. Just like today's lions and wolves, *Velociraptor* could kill bigger animals than itself. These dinosaurs hunted together.

Velociraptor

Fossil dung!

Dinosaur droppings also form fossils! These have pieces of food inside such as bones or plants. Some fossil droppings are as big as TV sets!

Coelophysis

Could dinosaurs leap and jump?

Scientists work out how dinosaurs moved by looking at their bones. The bones of *Coelophysis* are small, hollow, and light so it was probably able to dart about easily. The shapes of its teeth and jaw bones suggest that *Coelophysis* ate insects or fish.

Anatosaurus

Look

Look at some pictures of birds such as ostriches. Do they remind you of any dinosaurs in this book?

Why are some dinosaurs like birds?

Some dinosaurs had feathers, large eyes, and beaks. They even laid eggs and ate insects. It is believed that some changed (evolved) over time and became the very first birds on Earth.

Why did the dinosaurs die?

About 65 million years ago the dinosaurs suddenly died (became extinct). No one knows for sure why this happened, but something HUGE must have taken place to affect all life on the planet.

The dinosaurs may have been killed by a giant rock from space

Read

Go to the library to find out about animals today that are in danger of becoming extinct. Find out why.

What killed millions of animals?

Maybe volcanoes erupted, spitting out enormous clouds of ash and poisonous gas. Maybe a large lump of rock from space (a meteorite) smashed into the Earth. These things can change the weather, so perhaps the dinosaurs died because it got too cold for them.

Erupting volcanoes

Egg hunters!

Some dinosaurs might have become extinct because their eggs were eaten by other animals. Shrew-like creatures around at the time may have eaten the eggs at night as dinosaurs slept.

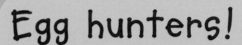

Could the dinosaurs have died from a disease?

This is unlikely because it wouldn't explain why so many millions of other animals died too. It is thought that more than two-thirds of all living things died at the same time as the dinosaurs, including sea creatures and plants.

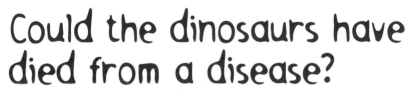

Can we find new dinosaurs?

The remains of animals and plants that lived long ago are called fossils. These remains are bones, teeth, eggs, and footprints— that have turned to rock over millions of years. Fossils of new dinosaurs such as *Jobaria* and *Janenschia* have been found in Africa.

Jobaria

Think

If you found fossils from a new dinosaur, think of what name you would give your own dinosaur.

Dino girl!

Leaellynasaura (lee-ell-in-oh-saw-ra) was named after the daughter of the scientists who found its fossils!

Leaellynasaura

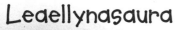

Janenschia

Where do scientists find dinosaur fossils?

Fossils are difficult to find because they are usually buried deep underground. Scientists look in places where layers of rock and soil have been removed by wind or water. At Dinosaur Cove the sea has washed away the rock, revealing the fossils of *Leaellynasaura*.

Could dinosaurs ever come back to life?

It is unlikely that dinosaurs will ever walk the Earth again. However, scientists are still finding fossils and using them to uncover new facts about the lives of these magnificent creatures. Dinosaurs live on, but only in our imaginations!

Quiz time

Do you remember what you have read about dinosaurs? These questions will test your memory. The pictures will help you. If you get stuck, read the pages again.

3. What were the biggest dinos?

page 10

4. What was the scariest dinosaur?

page 14

page 7

1. Why did dinosaurs eat stones?

5. What was the biggest meat-eating dinosaur?

page 15

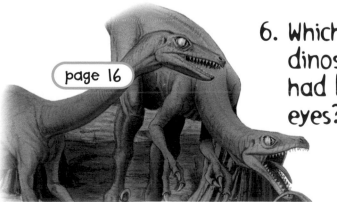

page 8

2. How big is a dinosaur tooth?

6. Which dinosaur had big eyes?

page 16

7. Were some dinosaurs small?

page 19

page 27

11. Why did the dinosaurs die?

8. Which dinosaur had a lumpy tail?

page 21

12. Where do scientists find dinosaur fossils?

page 29

13. Could dinosaurs ever come back to life?

9. Did dinosaurs look after their babies?

page 23

page 29

10. Could dinosaurs leap and jump?

page 25

Answers

1. To mash food up in their stomachs
2. Different sizes
3. Sauropods
4. Tyrannosaurus rex
5. Giganotosaurus
6. Troodon
7. Yes, some were not much bigger than pet cats
8. Euoplocephalus
9. Yes, some did
10. Yes, Coelophysis could
11. Volcanoes may have erupted, or a meteorite may have smashed into the Earth
12. In rocks
13. No

Index